Why Why Why are there schools in the sea?

Miles Kelly
PUBLISHING

First published in 2006 by
Miles Kelly Publishing Ltd
Bardfield Centre, Great Bardfield, Essex, CM7 4SL

2 4 6 8 10 9 7 5 3 1

Editorial Director
Belinda Gallagher

Art Director
Jo Brewer

Volume Designer
Michelle Cannatella

Indexer
Susan Bosanko

Production Manager
Elizabeth Brunwin

Reprographics
Anthony Cambray, Mike Coupe, Ian Paulyn

Character Cartoonist
Mike Foster

All other artworks from the Miles Kelly Archives

ISBN 1-84236-706-4

Printed in China

British Library Cataloguing-in-Publication Data
A catalogue record for this book is available
from the British Library

www.mileskelly.net
info@mileskelly.net

Contents

Is there only one big ocean? 4

Are there mountains under the sea? 5

Where do islands come from? 5

Do seashells have feet? 6

Can starfish grow arms? 6

When is a sponge like an animal? 7

Are there schools in the sea? 8

Which fish looks like an oar? 9

Do fish like to sunbathe? 9

What is the scariest shark? 10

Do some sharks use hammers? 11

When is a shark like a pup? 11

Who builds walls beneath the sea? 12

How do fish keep clean? 13

When is a fish like a clown? 13

What is the biggest sea animal? 14

Can whales sing songs? 15

Do whales grow tusks? 15

Do lions live in the sea? 16

Who sleeps in seaweed? 17

Can a walrus change colour? 17

Are there crocodiles in the sea? 18

Which lizard loves to swim? 19

How deep can a turtle dive? 19

Can seabirds sleep as they fly? 20

Do seabirds dig burrows? 21

Which bird dives for its dinner? 21

How do polar bears learn to swim? 22

Are penguins fast swimmers? 23

Which penguin dad likes to babysit? 23

Is seaweed good to eat? 24

How are lobsters caught? 25

Do pearls grow at sea? 25

Are there chimneys under the sea? 26

Do monsters live in the sea? 27

What is a mermaid? 27

How do divers breathe underwater? 28

Can people ride the waves? 29

What is a jetski? 29

Quiz time 30

Index 32

Is there only one big ocean?

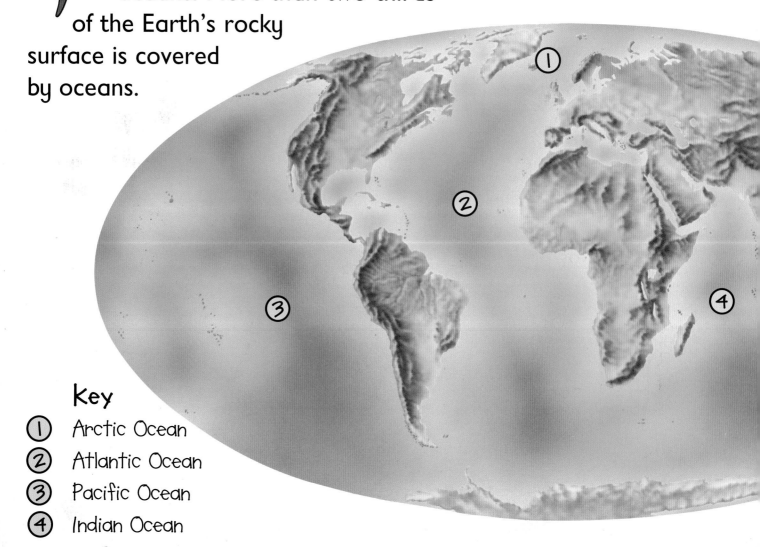

It seems that way. All the oceans flow into each other, but we know them as four different oceans – the Pacific, Atlantic, Indian and Arctic. The land we live on, the continents, rises out of the oceans. More than two-thirds of the Earth's rocky surface is covered by oceans.

Key

① Arctic Ocean
② Atlantic Ocean
③ Pacific Ocean
④ Indian Ocean

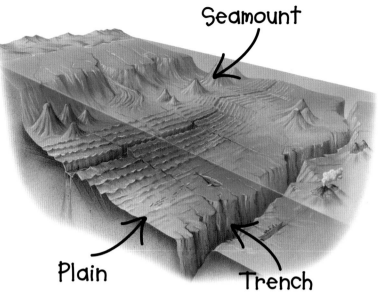

Seamount

Plain

Trench

Are there mountains under the sea?

Yes there are. The land beneath the sea is covered by mountains, flat areas called plains and deep valleys called trenches. There are also huge underwater volcanoes called seamounts.

Salty or fresh!

Almost all of the world's water is in the oceans. Only a tiny amount is in freshwater lakes and rivers.

Were do islands come from?

Islands are 'born' beneath the sea. If an underwater volcano erupts, it throws out hot, sticky lava. This cools and hardens in the water. Layers of lava build up and up, until a new island peeps above the waves.

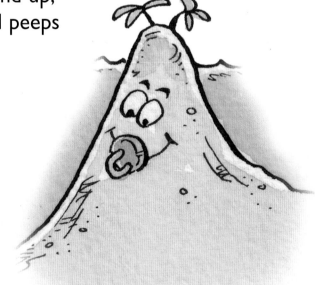

Look

Look at the world map to find where you live. Which ocean is nearest to you?

Do seashells have feet?

Tiny animals called limpets live inside some seashells. They stick to rocks at the shoreline where they eat slimy, green plants called algae. When the tide is out, limpets stick to the rocks like glue, with a strong muscular foot. They only move when the tide crashes in.

Can starfish grow arms?

Yes they can. Starfish may have as many as 40 arms, called rays. If a hungry crab grabs hold of one, the starfish abandons its arm, and uses the others to make its getaway. It then begins to grow a new arm.

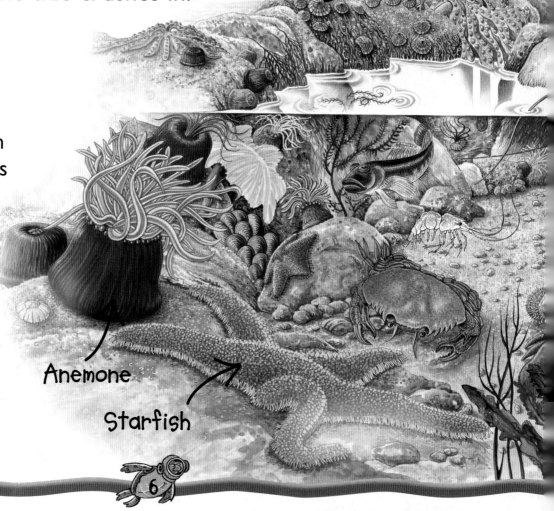

Limpets

Anemone

Starfish

6

Fighting fit!

Anemones are a kind of sea-living plant. Some anemones fight over their feeding grounds. Beadlet anemones shoot sharp, tiny hooks at each other until the weakest one gives in.

When is a sponge like an animal?

Sponges are animals! They are very simple creatures that filter food from sea water. The natural sponge that you use in the bath is a long-dead dried-out sponge!

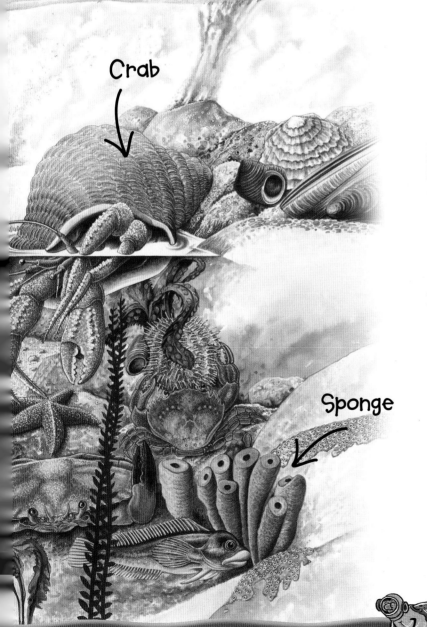

Crab

Sponge

Find

When you next visit a beach, try to find a rockpool. Write a list of what you see.

Are there schools in the sea?

Some fish live in big groups called schools. This may protect them from hungry hunters. There are thousands of different types of fish in the sea. Most are covered in shiny scales and use fins and tails to swim. Fish have gills that take in oxygen from the water so that they can breathe.

Read

What is a big group of fish called? Read this page to find out.

8

Which fish looks like an oar?

The oarfish does – and it can grow to be as long as four canoes! It is the longest bony fish and is found in all the world's oceans. Oarfish have a bright red fin along the length of their back. They swim upright through the water.

Oarfish

Flying high!

Flying fish cannot really fly. Fish can't survive out of water, but flying fish sometimes leap above the waves when they are swimming at high speed. They use their long fins to glide through the air for as long as 30 seconds.

Do fish like to sunbathe?

Sunfish like sunbathing. Ocean sunfish are huge fish that can weigh as much as one tonne – as heavy as a small car! They like to swim at the surface of the water, as if they're sunbathing.

School of fish

What is the scariest shark?

Great whites are the scariest sharks.
These huge fish speed through the
water at 30 kilometres an
hour. Unlike most fish, the
great white shark has warm blood. This allows
its muscles to work well but it also means that
it needs to eat lots of meat. Great white
sharks are fierce hunters. They will
attack and eat almost anything, but
prefer to feed on seals.

Great white shark

Draw
Using felt—tip
pens, draw your
own underwater
picture. Include a
great white shark.

Do some sharks use hammers?

Not really! Hammerhead sharks have hammer-shaped heads to search for food. With a nostril and an eye on each end of the 'hammer', they swing their heads from side to side, looking for a meal.

Hammerhead shark

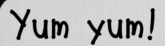

Yum yum!

Most sharks are meat eaters. Herring are a favourite food for sand tiger and thresher sharks, while a hungry tiger shark will gobble up just about anything!

When is a shark like a pup?

When it's a baby. Young sharks are called pups. Some grow inside their mother's body. Others hatch from eggs straight into the sea.

Who builds walls beneath the sea?

Tiny animals build underwater walls.
These walls are made of coral,
the leftover skeletons of tiny sea
animals called polyps. Over millions
of years, enough skeletons pile up to
form walls. These make a coral reef.
All kinds of creatures live around a reef.

Parrot fish

Seahorse

Look
Do you know
where the Great
Barrier Reef is?
Look in an atlas
to find out.

Clownfish

How do fish keep clean?

Cleaner wrasse are little fish that help other fish to keep clean! Larger fish, such as groupers and moray eels, visit the cleaner wrasse, which nibbles all the bugs and bits of dirt off the bigger fishes' bodies – what a feast!

Super reef

You can see the Great Barrier Reef from space! At over 2000 kilometres long, it is the largest thing ever built by living creatures.

Coral reef

Lionfish

Cleaner wrasse fish

When is a fish like a clown?

When it's a clownfish. These fish are brightly coloured, like circus clowns. They live among the stinging arms (tentacles) of the sea anemone. Clownfish swim among the stingers, where they are safe from enemies.

Sea anemone

What is the biggest sea animal?

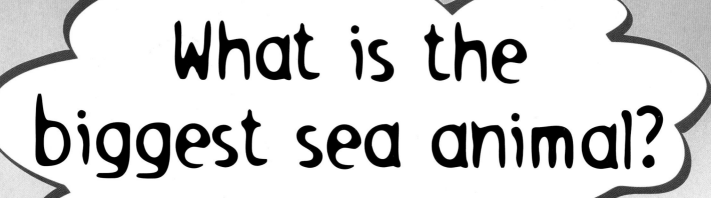

The blue whale is the biggest animal in the ocean – and the whole planet. It is about 30 metres long and can weigh up to 150 tonnes. It feeds on tiny, shrimp-like creatures called krill – and eats about four tonnes every day! Like other great whales, the blue whale has special, sieve-like parts in its mouth that are called baleen plates.

Blue whale

Can whales sing songs?

All whales make sounds, such as squeaks and moans. The humpback whale really does seem to sing. The males probably do this to attract a mate. He may repeat his song for up to 20 hours!

Humpback whale

Stick around!

Barnacles are shellfish. They attach themselves to ships, or the bodies of grey whales and other large sea animals.

Measure

The blue whale is 30 metres long. Can you measure how long you are?

Do whales grow tusks?

The narwhal has a tusk like a unicorn's. This tusk is a long, twirly tooth that comes out of the whale's head. The males use their tusks as weapons when they fight over females. The tusk can grow to 3 metres in length.

Do lions live in the sea?

There are lions in the sea, but not the furry, roaring kind. Sea lions, seals and walruses are all warm-blooded animals that have adapted to ocean life. They have flippers instead of legs — far more useful for swimming. A thick layer of fat under the skin keeps them warm in cold water.

Seal

Think
What do you think whales, dolphins and seals have in common with humans?

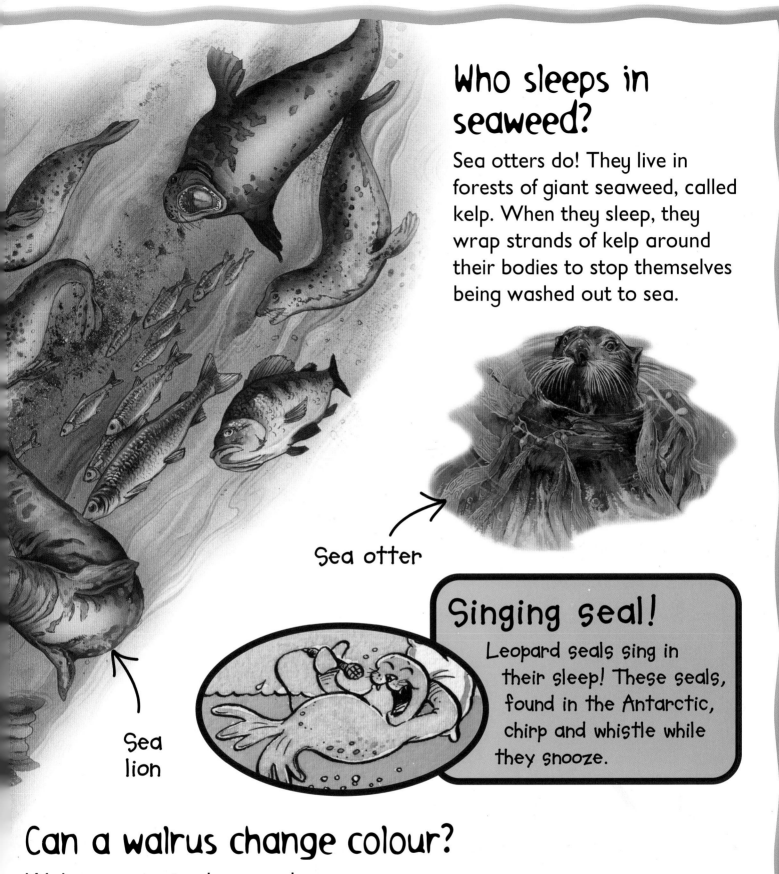

Who sleeps in seaweed?

Sea otters do! They live in forests of giant seaweed, called kelp. When they sleep, they wrap strands of kelp around their bodies to stop themselves being washed out to sea.

Sea otter

Sea lion

Singing seal!

Leopard seals sing in their sleep! These seals, found in the Antarctic, chirp and whistle while they snooze.

Can a walrus change colour?

Walruses seem to change colour. In cold water, a walrus can look pale brown or even white. This is because blood drains from the skin to stop the body losing heat. On land, blood returns to the skin and the walrus looks pink!

Are there crocodiles in the sea?

Most crocodiles live in rivers and swamps. The saltwater crocodile also swims out to sea – it doesn't seem to mind the salty water. These crocodiles are huge, and can grow to be 7 metres long and one tonne in weight.

Saltwater crocodile

Find out

Turtles only come ashore for one reason. Can you find out why?

Which lizard loves to swim?

Most lizards live on land, where it is easier to warm up their cold-blooded bodies. Marine iguanas depend on the sea for food. They dive underwater to eat seaweed growing on rocks. When they are not diving, they sit on rocks and soak up the sunshine.

How deep can a turtle dive?

Leatherback turtles can dive up to 1200 metres for their dinner. They are the biggest sea turtles and they make the deepest dives. Leatherbacks feed mostly on jellyfish but also eat crabs, lobsters and starfish.

Leatherback turtle →

Slithery snakes!

There are poisonous snakes in the sea. The banded sea snake and the yellow-bellied sea snake both use poison to kill their prey. Their poison is far stronger than that of land snakes.

Can seabirds sleep as they fly?

Wandering albatrosses are the biggest seabirds and spend months at sea. They are such good gliders that they even sleep as they fly. To feed, they sit on the surface of the water, where they catch creatures such as squid. An albatross has a wingspan of around 3 metres – about the length of a family car!

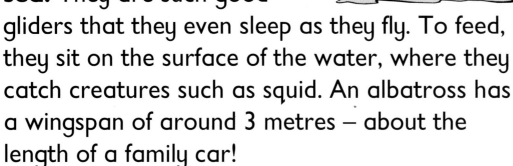

Wandering albatross

Think

Sea birds have webbed feet. Why do you think this is? Do you have webbed feet?

Do seabirds dig burrows?

Most seabirds make nests on cliffs.
The puffin digs a burrow on the clifftop, like a
rabbit. Sometimes, a puffin even takes
over an empty rabbit hole. Here it lays
its egg. Both parents look after the
chick when it hatches.

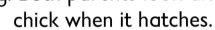

Puffins

Dancing birds!

Boobies are a type of seabird that
live in large groups. The males have
bright red or blue feet. When they
are looking for a mate, they dance in
front of the female, trying to attract
her with their colourful feet!

Which bird dives for its dinner?

The gannet dives headfirst into the
ocean to catch fish in its beak. It
dives at high-speed and hits the
water hard. Luckily, the gannet is
protected by cushions of air inside its
head that absorb most of the shock.

How do polar bears learn to swim?

Polar bears are good swimmers and they live around the freezing Arctic Ocean. They learn to swim when they are cubs, by following their mother into the water. With their big front paws, the bears paddle through the water. They can swim for many hours.

Polar bears

Imagine

Pretend to be a penguin. Imagine what life is like at the South Pole.

Are penguins fast swimmers?

Penguins are birds – but they cannot fly. All penguins are fast swimmers. The fastest swimmer is the gentoo penguin. It can reach speeds of 27 kilometres an hour underwater.

Gentoo penguin

Small and tall!

The smallest penguin is the fairy penguin at just 40 centimetres tall. The biggest is the emperor penguin at 1.3 metres in height – as tall as a seven-year-old child!

Which penguin dad likes to babysit?

Emperor penguin dads look after the baby chicks. The female lays an egg and leaves her mate to keep it warm. The penguin dad balances the egg on his feet to keep it off the freezing ice. He goes without food until the chick hatches. When it does, the mother returns and both parents look after it.

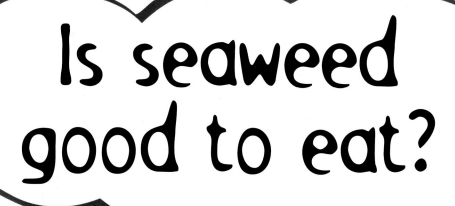

Is seaweed good to eat?

Seaweed can be very good to eat. In shallow, warm seawater, people can grow their own seaweed. It is then dried in the sun, which helps to keep it fresh. Seaweed is even used to make ice cream!

Growing seaweed

List

Make a list of the things you can eat that come from the ocean. Which of these things have you eaten before?

How do we get salt from the sea?

Sea water is salty. Salt is an important substance. In hot, low-lying areas, people build walls to hold shallow pools of sea water. The water dries up in the sun, leaving behind crystals of salt.

How are lobsters caught?

Lobsters are large shellfish that are good to eat. Fishermen catch them in wooden cages called pots. The lobsters are attracted to dead fish placed in the pots. They push the door of the pot open to get to the fish, but once inside, the lobster can't get out again.

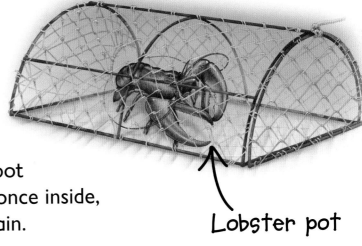

Lobster pot

Do pearls grow at sea?

Yes they do. Pearls grow inside oysters, a kind of shellfish. If a grain of sand gets stuck in an oyster's shell, it irritates its soft body. The oyster coats the grain with a substance that it uses to line the inside of its shell. In time, more coats are added and a pearl begins to form.

Are there chimneys under the sea?

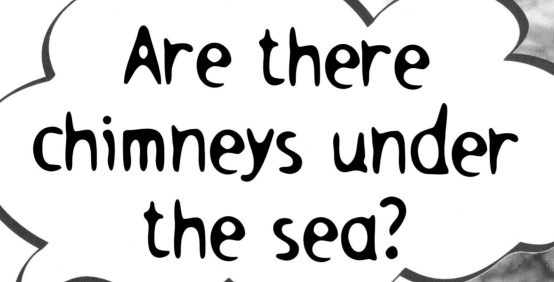

Rocky chimneys on the ocean floor give off clouds of hot water. These chimneys lie deep beneath the ocean. The hot water feeds strange creatures such as tube worms and sea spiders.

Rat tail fish

Watery village!

In 1963, diver Jacques Cousteau built a village on the bed of the Red Sea. Along with four other divers, he lived there for a whole month.

Giant clams

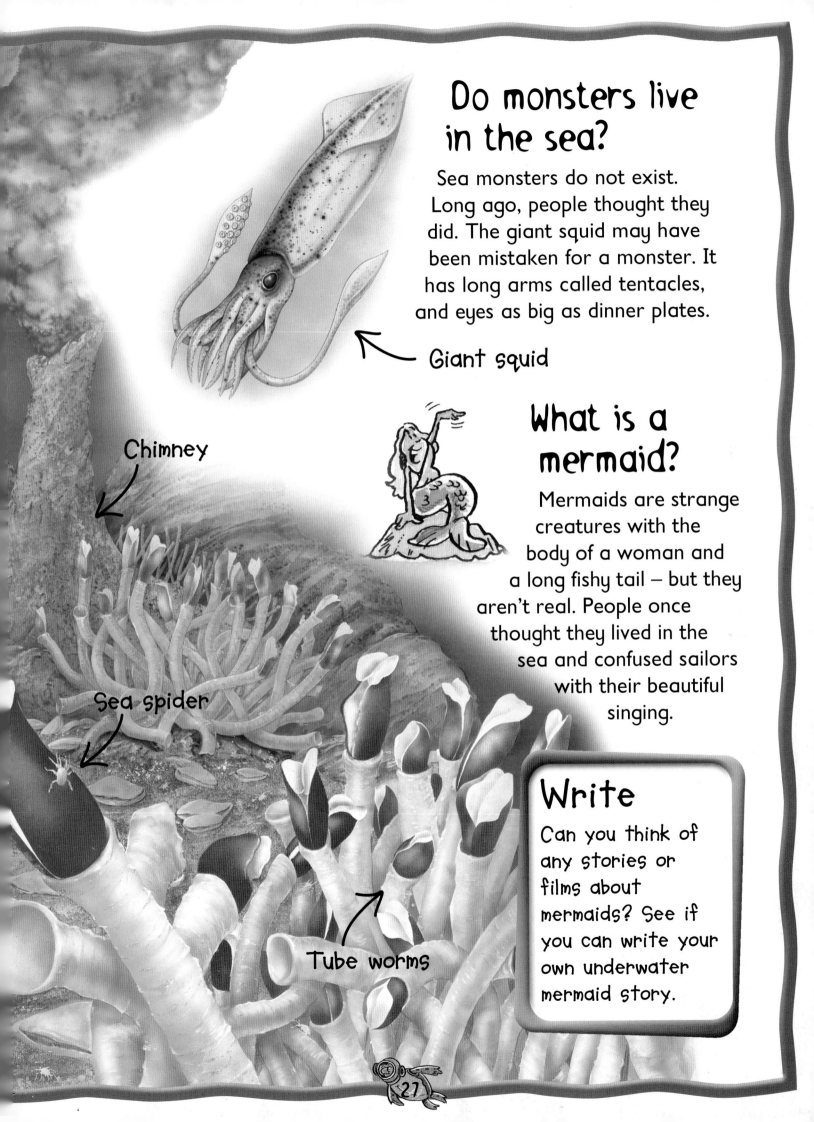

Do monsters live in the sea?

Sea monsters do not exist. Long ago, people thought they did. The giant squid may have been mistaken for a monster. It has long arms called tentacles, and eyes as big as dinner plates.

Giant squid

Chimney

Sea spider

What is a mermaid?

Mermaids are strange creatures with the body of a woman and a long fishy tail — but they aren't real. People once thought they lived in the sea and confused sailors with their beautiful singing.

Tube worms

Write

Can you think of any stories or films about mermaids? See if you can write your own underwater mermaid story.

How do divers breathe underwater?

Divers have a spare pair of lungs. Scuba divers carry a special piece of breathing equipment called an 'aqua lung'. These are tanks filled with oxygen (air) that sit on the divers' backs. A long tube supplies the diver with air.

Water record!

A single boat towed 100 waterskiers! This record was made off the coast of Australia in 1986 and no one has beaten it yet. The drag boat was a cruiser called 'Reef Cat'.

Can people ride the waves?

Yes they can, on surfboards. Surfing became popular in the 1950s. Modern surfboards are made of super-light material. People stand up on their boards and ride the waves. The best places to surf are off the coasts of Mexico and Hawaii.

Surfer

Aqua lung

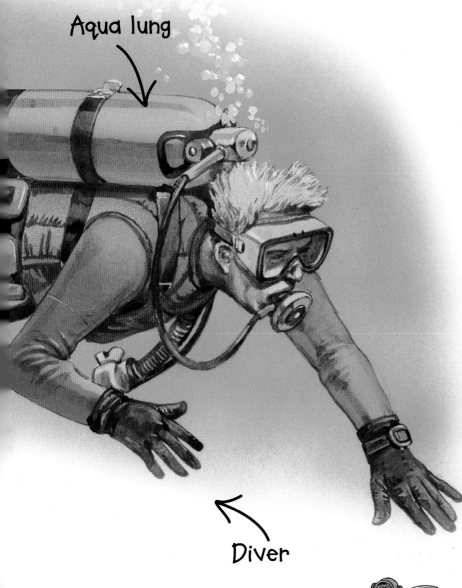

Diver

Wear

Try wearing some goggles in the bath. What can you see?

What is a jetski?

A jetski is like a motorbike without wheels that travels on water. It pushes out a jet of water behind it, which pushes it forward. Some jetskiers can reach speeds of 100 kilometres an hour.

Quiz time

page 9

Do you remember what you have read about oceans? Here are some questions to test your memory. The pictures will help you. If you get stuck, read the pages again.

3. Which fish looks like an oar?

4. Do some sharks use hammers?

page 11

1. Are there mountains under the sea?

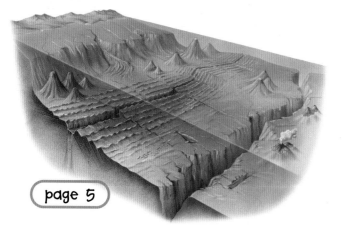

page 5

page 11

5. When is a shark like a pup?

2. When is a sponge like an animal?

page 7

page 17

6. Who sleeps in seaweed?

7. Are there crocodiles in the sea?

page 18

11. Is seaweed good to eat?

page 24

8. Can seabirds sleep as they fly?

page 20

12. What is a mermaid?

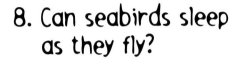

page 27

9. How do polar bears learn to swim?

page 22

page 28

13. How do divers breathe underwater?

10. Which penguin dad likes to babysit?

page 22

Answers

1. Yes, there are
2. A sponge is an animal
3. The oarfish
4. No, but the hammerhead shark has a hammershaped head
5. When it's a baby – young sharks are called pups
6. The sea otter
7. The saltwater crocodile swims in the sea
8. Yes, the wandering albatross can
9. By following their mother into the water
10. The emperor penguin
11. Yes, it can be
12. A creature that is half-woman, half-fish
13. By using an aqua lung

Index

A
albatrosses 20
algae 6
anemones 7, 13
animals 6, 7, 12, 14–15, 16–17, 18–19, 22
aqua lungs 28
Arctic Ocean 4, 22
arms 6
Atlantic Ocean 4

B
baleen plates 14
banded sea snakes 19
barnacles 15
beadlet anemones 7
birds 20–21, 23
blue whales 14–15
boats 28
boobies 21
breathing 8, 28
burrows 21

C
chimneys 26
clams 26
cleaner wrasse 13
clownfish 13
colouring 9, 17, 21
continents 4
coral reefs 12–13
Cousteau, Jacques 26
crabs 6, 19
crocodiles 18

D
dancing 21
digging 21
diving and divers 19, 21, 26, 28–29
drag boats 28

E
eels 13
eggs 11, 21, 23
emperor penguins 23

F
fairy penguins 23
feet 6, 20, 21
fighting 7, 15
fish 8–9, 10–11, 13, 21, 26
flippers 16
flying fish 9
food and feeding 6, 7, 10, 11, 14, 19, 20, 21, 23, 24, 25, 26
fresh water 5

G
gannets 21
gentoo penguins 23
giant clams 26
giant squid 27
gills 8
goggles 29
Great Barrier Reef 12, 13
great whales 14–15
great white sharks 10
groupers 13

H, I
hammerhead sharks 11
humpback whales 15
iguanas 19
Indian Ocean 4
islands 5

J, K
jetskis 29
kelp 17
krill 14

L
lava 5
leatherback turtles 19
leopard seals 17
limpets 6
lionfish 13
lobsters 19, 25

M, N
marine iguanas 19
mermaids 27
moray eels 13
mountains 5
narwhals 15

O
oarfish 9
ocean floor 5, 26
ocean sunfish 9
oxygen 8, 28
oysters 25

P
Pacific Ocean 4
parrot fish 12
pearls 25
penguins 22, 23
plains 5
plants 6, 7
polar bears 22
polyps 12
puffins 21
pups 11

R
rat tail fish 26
rays 6
Red Sea 26
reefs 12–13
reptiles 18–19

S
salt 25
saltwater crocodiles 18
sand tiger sharks 11
schools of fish 8
scuba divers 28
sea anemones 7, 13
sea lions 16
sea monsters 27
sea otters 17
sea snakes 19
sea spiders 26, 27
sea water 5, 7, 18, 24, 25
seabirds 20–21, 23
seahorses 12
seals 10, 16, 17
seamounts 5
seaweed 17, 19, 24
sharks 10–11
shellfish 6, 15, 19, 25, 26
sleeping 17, 20
songs 15, 17, 27
sponges 7
squid 20, 27
starfish 6, 19
surfing 29
swimming 9, 10, 16, 18, 19, 22, 23

T
tentacles 13, 27
thresher sharks 11
tiger sharks 11
trenches 5
tube worms 26, 27
turtles 18, 19
tusks 15

U, V
underwater village 26
volcanoes 5

W
walruses 16, 17
wandering albatrosses 20
waterskiing 28
whales 14–15
wingspans 20

Y
yellow-bellied sea snakes 19